# THE FOREVER PARENTING PROJECT

## A MOTHER'S STORY
### EFFECTIVE WAYS TO ENJOY PARENTING YEARS WITH YOUR TEENAGER

GLORIA B. LEWIS

BK Royston Publishing
www.bkroystonpublishing.com

Cover Design: Elite Covers
ISBN-13: 978-1-959543-47-3

Printed in the United States of America

# Gratitudes

*To my sons Dedric, Lance & Denver, my three heartbeats. I am proud of you!*
*To my parents and their parents, who did the best they could with what they had.*

# CONTENTS

INTRODUCTION                                                                    1

ABOUT THE AUTHOR                                                               5

CHAPTER 1: *Being a Parent Is the Hardest Job in the World*                    7

CHAPTER 2: *My Parenting Journey*                                             13

CHAPTER 3: *Parenting Styles and Parenting Skills*                           21

CHAPTER 4: *How to Parent with Awareness and Courage*                        29

CHAPTER 5: *Family Communication and Age Gap*                                37

CHAPTER 6: *Family Love Language and Birth Order*                            51

CHAPTER 7: *Family Boundaries and Expectations*                              59

CONCLUSION                                                                    69

# INTRODUCTION

Are you ever curious about how young adults' parents survive their teenage years? Do you visualize your teen doing all the right things according to you, but their behavior is out of sync? I want to help parents see where they are in their parenting journey, explore the parenting skills that are not working, and share practical suggestions and helpful tips.

But first, let me tell my story.

I am the grateful mother of three sons. I started this journey of helping families out of my need to be a better parent. I began searching for anything that would offer a supportive framework for becoming the mother my sons deserved.

After researching and reading books and magazines on parenting, I was motivated to seek out opportunities to volunteer for family education programs. By doing this, I saw it as a way of helping myself be consistent in my new way of parenting and learning new parenting skills.

My parenting struggles began after I married, had my second son, and lived as part of a blended family. I noticed my parenting style had changed somewhat since having my firstborn child. At the time, I did not realize that it related to the seven-year age gap of my boys. It was not until my firstborn entered junior high school and I gave birth to my third son, creating another age gap of six years, that I began to feel the stress and the need to parent differently.

Some adolescent issues with my firstborn that were occurring and strained our family dynamics were expressing himself through anger (non-communication, negative overtone, unhappy disposition) daily. Since this was my first experience as a parent to a teenager, I had to learn how to parent an adolescent, find out what I needed to do, and what I needed to avoid doing to deal with the highs and lows of his adolescent behavior. In doing this, I knew I would have to be a better communicator and let go of judgment, perfectionism, and unrealistic expectations.

My parents did not practice open communication in our home, and I was not encouraged to share my thoughts or concerns, good or bad, without the worry of non-supportive feedback. What did this look and feel like for me as a child? Fear, rejection, and I did not matter. What did this look and feel like as I matured? Fear of rejection, low self-esteem, lack of self-confidence, and resistance to asking for help.

So, as I began to have my own family, I knew open communication would be significant for me. I did not know what challenges came with it, nor did I have a blueprint for making it happen. But I was confident in my desire and abilities to build a loving child-parent relationship by being an attentive listener with an open heart and mind. My goal is to help and encourage all parents to enjoy their parenting years and not feel alone in this parenting journey. Parenting is forever!

Today, I inspire some and give permission to others to create new boundaries and expectations, identify personal parenting styles, learn how to flow with life changes, and effectively communicate.

Although I speak from the perspective of parenting teenagers in this book, you will clearly see that the strategies, suggestions, and parenting tips can be adjusted to parent all school-age children.

## What you will learn from my book:

By the end of this book, you will have clarity on your parenting style and what works best for your family dynamics.

You will know how to effectively communicate with your teen and other family members, creating less stress.

## This book is not for...

- Those who believe parent education is not necessary.
- Those who are comfortable with the status quo: i.e., not wanting to make a change.
- Those who like to make excuses.
- Those who desire to remain stuck.

## This book is for...

- Those who are willing to learn.
- Those who have been stuck, but have a desire to break through that ceiling.
- Those who are willing to recognize that what is holding you back doesn't have to any longer.

Those who have a desire to master parenting basics.

# ABOUT THE AUTHOR

Gloria considers herself a life-long learner. She writes and leads groups through the perspective of a mother who has made the paradigm shift from traditional to positive parenting. Gloria delights in sharing her journey with others and inspiring families to choose to be empathetic and a good listener and how to embrace the vulnerabilities and humility that come with parenting. She has independently researched and studied various parenting programs during her parenting journey. She strives to continue to learn and expand her knowledge of family education, and every family she has the opportunity to help grow. She is the grateful mother to three sons.

"*Parenting is the easiest thing in the world to have an opinion about, but the hardest thing in the world to do.*"

—— MATT WALSH

# CHAPTER 1

# BEING A PARENT IS THE HARDEST JOB IN THE WORLD

---

## Parent with Confidence

This book is part memoir and part self-help. It is my personal story about parenting teenagers. It is me informing and giving valuable advice and wisdom to readers on being creative with their parenting strategies. I share stories about my role as a mother raising teenagers, three sons with a 13-year age gap between oldest and youngest, and the processes and strategies I used. Although I talk of how these strategies work for teens, they can be adjusted to parent children of all ages. I provide practical tools that can be easily used in any family dynamic, creating an overall happy parent every day. I am writing this parenting book to reflect and make sense of my life journey as a parent and my emotional confusion, to reflect on lessons learned and inspire other parents to become aware of their emotional wounds, and to choose to heal as they attempt to raise emotionally healthy children.

This book creates awareness around "Parenting Is Forever" as my sons became more independent and eventually made me an empty nester. I realize I was still parenting just on a different level for a different stage of their life, young adult to adulthood.

In reality, I am still their mom, "The Parent." I realize I will still be giving parental guidance, just not so much "on-demand" but on a "need to know" basis and on occasion "on request."

Here are some parenting truths I have learned: Parenting is forever; parents can have a satisfying relationship with their children during their teen years; and parents can enjoy their parenting years amid the family-life chaos.

## Me as a Parent Educator

I became interested in parent education during a time I felt my parenting experience with raising my first teenage child was traumatizing for me when I was age 35. So, no matter what stage or age you are at in your parenting journey, redirecting yourself and your family is never too late.

Don't pressure yourself to be perfect; that adds more stress and anxiety to your parenting role. Enjoy the journey and focus on the processes and strategies that bring calm, joy, peace, and love into your family space.

## Parent as a Great Communicator

Effective communication creates trusting relationships. Only through awareness of effective communication can the cycle of miscommunication within families end. In chapter 5, I will be discussing family communication in detail, but here I want to shine a light of awareness on how we as the parent set the tone for how our families communicate. To start being a great parent communicator, I suggest you establish a daily focus routine of intentional moments that nurtures genuine communication between family members. Each child is unique; here is a simple form of awareness I found helpful. Speak at their age level. In my experience growing up, my parents communicated with my siblings and me alike, despite our age and maturity level. Nurturing the habit of communicating with your child at his or her age level creates an environment for you to see them as themselves. Here are the age groups I suggest you follow:

Birth to age 5 is an opportunity to show how you want your child to communicate. Ages 6 to 11 are an opportunity to encourage consistent communication.

Ages 12 to 18 are an opportunity to strengthen your muscles for being patient and calm, encouraging attentive listening while being firm and respectful.

You can never start too soon or too late in teaching effective communication.

## Our Parenting Environments

During the years I was a parent facilitator, I met a very diverse group of parents, and they all had their reasoning for parenting the way they parent, even those that knew they lacked parenting skills. Many were very open in sharing their reasons for being tired and frustrated with parenting their child; some even admitted they had given up hope and welcomed the parent training offered.

Here is a list of types of parents I have observed and encountered over the years:

- Hit and miss — parent too early, lack parenting skills
- Think they know — attach to the power and control
- Going off instinct — no effort outside of self
- Traditional parenting — fearful of change, societal norm, familiarity
- Opposite of their parents — resulted in being too strict or overprotective

My intention for readers as they read my story is that they become more confident in their parenting skills, embrace parent education, trust their intuition, and welcome the opportunity when it presents itself to share experiences and receive resources.

## Parent with Family Goals in Mind

One great parenting goal is to create an environment where your teenager will feel supported and empowered to talk to you and other responsible and trusted adults in his or her life.

Being a parent educator, I have a lot of resources at my disposal. Over the years, I used them to better myself and share with others. My inspiration for being a better parent has always been my three sons. They deserve a good mom, and I tried to be that for them as best as possible before they went out into that big, big world. What I have found to be the most challenging about being a parent is seeing my children experience failure disappointment and watching them go through that phase where they act as if they are invincible.

Another excellent parenting goal is for your teen to know the value of family structure and the correct expression of emotions and to be well versed in social and life skills.

To accomplish this, parents must parent confidently while their children are in their household to create empowered children who are emotionally and behaviorally mature.

What I know for certainty is parenting is not easy for anyone and that it does take a village (collective efforts).

As a parent, I believe we are all doing the best we can with the information we have, but there comes a time when we need a fresh approach and new information to help us enjoy our parenting years because parenting is forever.

## How to Use this Book

This book is a tool to help you have awareness about practical parenting tools, strategies, and ideas to help strengthen your parenting skills. My goal is to provide a structure for your being consistent and confident in choosing the strategies that work best for your family dynamic.

The best benefit you can get from reading this book is to better understand your teenager and confidently embrace your own personal growth. Throughout the chapters, you will find reflection questions to help you connect more to the topics of discussion. I encourage you to take the time to give serious thought and contemplation to each question as it relates to your parenting goals.

"*Children thrive in a variety of family forms. They normally develop with single parents, unmarried parents, multiple caretakers, and traditional two-parent families. What children require is loving and attentive adults, not a particular family type.*"

— SANDRA SCARR

# CHAPTER 2
# MY PARENTING JOURNEY

## My Parenting Style Initially as a Single Mom

As a single mom at age 21, I started parenting in a strict mode. Why? Out of familiarity. I was familiar with expecting my child to do what I say, "because I said so." But the more and more I responded to my child in this matter, I began to reflect on how that parenting behavior made me feel when I was a child. As the eldest of five children, I did not feel seen, I did not feel I was enough, and I did not feel heard. My parents regularly reminded me, "You are the oldest; you should know better," or "Your siblings are watching you — do not do that." As a child, hearing my parents say this made me think they were asking me to be responsible for my siblings' behavior. When I was a child, and even throughout my teen years, this was an unrealistic expectation of my parents. This is not to cast blame or judgment on my parents and how they parent; this is me reflecting. Out of my frustration with how they parented, I understood that my parents parented the way my grandparents parented them, meaning they were doing the best they could. I learned this early on in my childhood and succumbed to their controlling behavior. Eventually, I became resentful, angry, and outspoken in my teen years, which led me to be observant and curious of how other adults parent.

During my angry teen years, I often wondered why my parents did not put effort into parenting differently. I want to believe that they did try, but the challenge must have been the deep conditioning of the societal norm. My curiosity about parenting started me to think differently from my parents.

## My Parenting Style After Marriage

I was age 28 when I married, had been a single mom for seven years by then, and shortly after, I was expecting my second child. My second born was so different from my first that I felt like I could take a breather from my new parenting practices. Still, during these years of parenting two children, I noticed I would have to adjust family rules to be age-appropriate as there was a seven-year age difference. This was a light bulb moment because I felt the stress of parenting and being a working mom and wife. At this point of my journey, I was parenting differently but felt my way by doing what made my life flow more smoothly. Making limited demands, delegating, and having my firstborn be responsible for household chores (this was new for him).

My parenting fears increased when I became the parent of two children. Here are a few of the parenting fears I had over the years: health (sick from daycare, ear infections, allergies, eating habits), socially awkward, bullied, hurt (sports injuries, car accidents, abuse), being friendly with strangers, entitlement behavior.

I was intentional about not projecting my fears onto my sons through the years. It was a juggling act with my emotions for years because my parenting fears were so intense. I wanted to be in a space where I could demonstrate and communicate these awarenesses without causing my children to fear.

To reduce my anxiety, it took me learning how to be patient with myself and acknowledge the emotions I had attached to my parenting fears and why. I later knew it was some of my childhood fears showing up in the way I parent.

Being a parent requires us to be that responsible adult who trains and prepares our children how to make good choices and how to respond to the environment outside our home.

Over the years, as I would inform my sons on what to expect related to my parenting fears list above, they would shrug it off as "mom, you worry too much." I was okay with that response because my job as a parent is to make sure they know how to respond to any situation. How else would they know?

At age 34, I gave birth to my third child, but while he was still in my womb, I knew I needed to be more creative with my parenting style because I now have another age gap of six years.

# *Children Learn What They Live*

## by Dorothy Law Nolte, Ph.D.

If children live with criticism, they learn to condemn.
If children live with hostility, they learn to fight.
If children live with ridicule, they learn to be shy.
If children live with shame, they learn to feel guilty.

If children live with encouragement, they learn confidence.
If children live with tolerance, they learn to be patient.
If children live with praise, they learn to appreciate.
If children live with acceptance, they learn to love.
If children live with approval, they learn to like themselves.
If children live with honesty, they learn truthfulness.
If children live with security, they learn to have faith in themselves and others.

If children live with friendliness, they learn the world is a nice place in which to live.

This is the author-approved short version.

I love, love, love this poem. I kept it on my refrigerator. When I first became aware of it, I became overwhelmed with emotions. It felt burdensome as if it added duties onto my already hectic parenting schedule, but over time as I embraced them one and two at a time, I saw the beauty in parenting with awareness.

## Question to Self During This Phase of My Life:

What is my parenting mission?

_____

_____

_____

_____

What is my parenting philosophy now that I have more children/our family is growing?

_____

_____

_____

_____

How do I incorporate this into my everyday interaction with my children?

_____

_____

_____

_____

## My Search on How to Parent Differently — the Challenges

After giving birth to my third son, not only was I feeling overwhelmed with all things family, but my firstborn also was, apparently. He was becoming rebellious.

Although this behavior is part of teenage development, I was not prepared emotionally or mentally to deal with this daily. Two things I knew I needed to be intentional about were being a better communicator and practicing patience with him and myself.

I became interested in parent education when I felt my parenting experience with raising my first teenage child was traumatizing for me. After he graduated from high school, I felt like I could catch my breath. I began searching for a parenting program/class/group that I could be a part of to help reinforce my new parenting skills. Also, so I could be better prepared for my next teenage-child experience. I wanted to help parents in the same situation as I had been parenting a teenager for the first time with multi-age children and to share my challenges, experiences, and resources.

The result of my search was a nonprofit truancy program that offered services to parents and families. I wanted to serve, guide, and help parents with information and resources that would assist them through their child's teenage-child years — to let them know they are not in the struggle alone.

I spent more than five years with this program as a group facilitator teaching court-ordered parent and youth classes to a diverse group of families. I fell in love with what the program offered, which was based on the Search Institute Developmental Assets® Framework. During this time, I realized from a different perspective that effective parenting requires community support. I taught my classes in a way that made parents feel safe to ask questions, share their stories, and ask for additional help outside of the class/program. During this time, my children were the ages of 7, 13, and 19, and I was still recovering from my first teenage-child years.

## Focus on Creating Memories and Family Traditions

Family memories can make family life meaningful and create strong family bonds, fun, and traditions. I like to call them "family magic moments."

I enjoy creating memories and reflecting on things from the past through pictures. I am the photographer in my family. I always enjoyed seeing photos of my parents and grandparents when they were younger and how they lived before me. So, this is a hobby that I incorporated into my family dynamics. Over the years, my children have enjoyed having access to the many family photo albums I have created. As for family traditions, one of my sons became fascinated with family tree history thanks to a third-grade school project. This led to his asking lots of questions about my grandparents and beyond. I eventually created our family tree to help me answer his questions, and, finally, we got to participate in our family reunion celebration on my dad's side of the family. Traditions like these help our children see and feel their family connection through the years. Other suggestions you might want to try to make are a family history scrapbook, family timeline, or family time capsule. Whatever new family tradition you try, remember to have fun.

## When I Began to Enjoy My Parenting Years

I did not feel the rhythm or flow in my parenting journey until my firstborn's senior year. I had not started facilitating parenting classes at this time, but I had done a lot of reading and researching parenting and adolescents.

I stand by my story "I was traumatized" by my firstborn teenage experience. Why? Because I was not prepared in any way for this adolescent behavior and the roller coaster of emotions that came with it. The struggle was intensified by my own personal suppressed emotions from my childhood and my current life stresses.

After receiving his high school diploma, he began to live out his life on his terms. I began to reflect on what I had learned and failed miserably at parenting my first teen. Also, during this

time, I had to learn to let go of judgment, criticism, perfectionism, unrealistic expectations and to practice patience. When he was in eighth grade, I began this, meaning it was not an overnight process. I had to unlearn some behaviors, including being a yeller.

At this stage of my parenting, I was in burnout mode. I felt emotionally drained from the years of carpooling to multiple schools, after-school activities, learning to parent differently, understanding the development of adolescents, how to parent boys, and maintaining a healthy marriage and work life. Whew! So, with my next teen two years later, I knew I needed to be firmer and more consistent with my new way of parenting if I wanted to parent with less stress.

I began to enjoy my parenting years after I survived my first teen experience. After my reflections, I intentionally minimized my stress level as a parent. That required me to inform my family of my new consistent way of running our household. One of my biggest struggles was the age gap between my three sons. My strategies of change were my communication patterns and how I managed my emotions.

This adjustment in my parenting style started me on a parenting journey with a sense of awareness and less stress creating a better connection with my sons. I see parenting as a path for guiding children and creating an environment for safe family communication.

I am passionate about how much my parenting style has helped me in my parenting journey, and I am here now to share the parenting tools, strategies, and resources I used with you.

*"When awareness is your reality, you don't need to explain your shortcomings or missed opportunities."*

—— WAYNE DYER

# CHAPTER 3
# PARENTING STYLES AND PARENTING SKILLS

## Parenting Styles

I knew what kind of parent I would be when I had my first child at age 21. Unlike my parents, I wanted my children to have some control and ownership in their lives, including open communication, something I did not experience from my parents.

At the time, I was not aware of parenting styles or that there were various ways to parent a child, and I just felt that my way of parenting would be the opposite of my childhood experience with my parents. In hindsight, I knew they were doing what they knew to do as they were young parents themselves.

I now know that there are various parenting styles, and I will briefly describe them and the expected behavior of the child.

1. **Authoritarian Parenting** (giving orders): strict, inflexible, high expectations, punishes rather than discipline. **Behavior of child(ren):** struggle with learning to think for themselves, rebel, go along with (controlling behavior of parent).

2. **Permissive Parenting** (giving in): nurturing, affectionate, few or inconsistent boundaries, the role of a friend rather than a parent. **Behavior of child(ren):** little self-control, trouble with relationships and the rights of others.

3. **Authoritative Parenting** (giving choices): nurturing, affectionate, set clear boundaries, disciplines through guidance, open communication. **Behavior of child(ren)**: more cooperative, better self-esteem, focus on positive virtue and praise.

4. **Uninvolved Parenting** (fulfill child's basic needs): emotionally detached, self-absorbed, inconsistent or with no boundaries, and has little interaction. **Behavior of child(ren)**: lack self-control and have low self-esteem.

## Questions to Self

Do you recognize your parenting style? Do you see your child's behavior in the list above?

_____

_____

_____

_____

_____

Have you ever thought about why we all don't parent in the same way? How do you parent now?

_____

_____

_____

_____

_____

## Awareness of Your Parenting Style

Being aware means being aware of something and understanding what's happening around you. It can also be something you feel, experience, or observe.

Hopefully, you have identified your current parenting style and you are ready to know the four main benefits of parenting with awareness: promotes more parental involvement, improves parent-child communication and connection, lowers stress and anxiety, and minimizes feelings of depression.

My intention here is to help parents be aware of their awareness when it comes to parenting. For instance, be mindful of how you respond and react (voice tone, body language, words), the feelings of your teenager, and yourself daily. Being an aware parent is knowing and understanding a lot about what is happening to your child and yourself physically, emotionally, and mentally.

I often became so involved in doing all the things I thought were considered being a good mom that I wasn't aware of my thought process and how it affected how I responded and reacted to my son's annoying behavior.

I eventually observed myself being the parent who yells. As a yeller, I communicated loudly and went on long rants. I had migraine headaches, which I later discovered were from my stressful lifestyle (overwhelm, burnout, frustration). There are various reasons we yell at our children; it will happen at some point in our parenting journey, but you need to know that yelling is considered a harmful strategy for communication. I do not recall my parents being yellers, but on several occasions, they felt the need to use harsh tones to get the desired behavior from my siblings and me. I have since learned that my childhood memory of not feeling seen is one of the things that influenced my yelling. Therefore, when my children would not respond to me promptly, I would be triggered to yell, causing me to be seen and heard.

I could be cooking in the kitchen and just in tune with my own negative and repetitive thoughts, but in the background, I heard the annoying aggravation of my boys with each other. Instead of snapping out of my repetitive thought process, I would yell and threaten, and to no avail; the aggravation continued. At that moment, I stopped what I was doing to attend to the matter but wondered why I did not attend to the annoyance sooner. I later realized that I was in another space with my thoughts while my boys terrorized one another.

I caught myself doing this on several occasions, locked in a negative thought cycle relating to my stresses in life and responding to my children with yelling and threats. I soon realized I let my emotions control my reaction to my family's weekly after-school chaos.

At this stage of my parenting, I started to feel my suppressed emotions come through my communication with my sons. I did not know much about healthy ways of expressing emotions, mainly because suppressed emotions were the norm in my childhood environment.

I had many days of frustration from them not responding to my yelling. I remember one day being so stressed and tired from my yelling that I caught myself and said to myself, "You are doing too much to get them to respond." I began asking myself why I felt the need to yell. At that moment, I realized it was my children's behavior and the stress I was carrying from my unresolved family issues and unhealthy personal relationships.

So, on my pathway to change from being a yeller to being a clear communicator, I had to step into self-accountability and take care of my emotional needs. Our job as parents includes being responsible for our teenagers' safety and managing our emotions.

This transition from a yeller led me to self-monitoring my tone. It was not an overnight change, but I kept at it because I felt better in my body, and my family began to respond to me more positively. I share this part of my parenting journey because it was me getting clear on how I was parenting and understanding the parenting styles that helped me see what was not working for me and what other options were available. Rather than yelling, pause, breathe deeply, talk about how you feel, and address the behavior calmly but firmly before you react. There will be no need for threats. Make the consequences clear.

## Question to Self:

Do you ever question your behavior as a parent? Do you have a self-talk practice?

_____

_____

_____

_____

_____

_____

What's your tone like when you respond to your children?

_____

_____

_____

_____

Knowing your parenting style is vital to raising responsible children. A reminder of parenting styles: authoritarian, permissive, authoritative, and uninvolved. In addition to parental LOVE having respect, empathy, creativity, and flexibility in your parenting style is key to its effectiveness.

Good parenting does not come; naturally, it requires patience in finding your parenting style. Give yourself time to learn/practice the skill with your family and expect some resistance but if you "the parent" trust that your new parent skill is ideal, stick with it and realize that sometimes change takes more time than you want. Be patient.

Please note that there are various reasons why families display different parenting styles, such as the difference in culture, personality, family size, parental background, socioeconomic status, educational level, and religion.

When determining the best parenting style for yourself and your family, go with the one that would complement your family values and produce effective results like respectful, responsible, and resilient children. Also, I encourage you to be confident in your ability to combine both parents' parenting styles to create your unique parenting style for your family dynamics.

## Let's Talk About My Parenting Style and How I Settled into It

I consider myself an authoritative parent with a mix of love and logic, which is the opposite of my parents, who displayed the authoritarian parenting style.

As I settled into this parenting style, I became confident with my abilities and my way of communicating with my little human beings. I focused on open communication, offering options, asking questions, giving feedback, and being empathetic I created an environment where they could balance being emotionally intelligent, respectful, responsible, and effective communicators.

What parenting goals have you set for your family?

What are the outcomes you are expecting?

Give yourself permission to create parenting goals that allow you to parent in a way that produces cooperative, responsible, and happy children — in turn, having responsible adults who can cope in the world.

## Parenting Skills

Parents of teenagers should maintain five basic parenting skills to effectively parent: encouragement, can do, choices, self-control, and respecting feelings. Encouragement nurtures self-esteem in teens and builds parent and child trust. Can do is where the parent teaches teen acceptable behavior, and choices are where parent and child work together to solve problems and make decisions. I am sure you know by now that parenting is a process, and change is gradual. If these basic skills are not as strong as they should be at this stage of your parenting, be patient with yourself and create a plan.

It is our responsibility as parents to change and grow to meet the needs of our teens. This awareness started me on my journey of parenting differently and focusing on my self-growth. Initially, it was challenging and even confusing for my children and me, but once I started seeing the positive benefits of the change, I knew I needed to stick to my new way of parenting.

## Teachable Moments

My revamped parenting style became known to me as "teachable moments." When I mentioned earlier about being a yeller and ranting? Well, it was during this transition of my monitoring my parent-voice (tone) that I sought out a more peaceful and calm way to have a rant about inappropriate behavior or choices.

Teachable moments became a light bulb moment when all my boys were of age, and our family schedule and daily activities were hectic. They were all at a stage in their young lives where it seemed as if I was always giving directives and redirecting, and they were their usual un-adult selves by ignoring me or blowing me off as saying, "here we go again." Well, it began to take a stressful toll on me. It then became evident that I was at a stage of my parenting where I needed to re-evaluate how I was communicating and adjust my parenting strategy accordingly. This re-evaluation occurred every two to three years based on each son's grade level/academic school year.

There were many opportunities where my boys felt the need to lie, and when they did, it was another "teachable moment" for me. The discussion would be about being truthful, making the right choices, and how their actions affect them and others (life skill lesson). Although I would be upset and disappointed, I immediately saw this as an opportunity to go on my rant in my

parent-calm voice about being truthful and to ask why they felt the need to lie. During this time, I would observe their emotion behind the lie (fear, guilt, not thinking).

Another strategy I used during these moments was to put myself in their situation and try to view things from their teen worldview. Sometimes I would get the why, but other times I had to conclude they just were not thinking.

I eventually got good at detecting opportunities for "teachable moments" consistently, and I also became comfortable with the idea of addressing only the son that created the teachable moment. This was a big deal for me because when I was a child, when one of my siblings made a lousy choice, the majority of the time we all suffered the consequences.

## Question to Self:

How often do you notice opportunities to teach your child a life lesson or life skill?

_____

_____

_____

_____

_____

_____

"*Parenting is a lifetime job and does not stop when a child grows up.*"

—— JAKE SLOPE

# CHAPTER 4

# HOW TO PARENT WITH AWARENESS AND COURAGE

---

## During My Early Parenting Years (first 13 years)

I was my parents (authoritarian), but I was trying to break away from that way of being, but it was challenging because it was all I knew. I had guilt for wanting to parent differently, and I feared my parent's judgment and feedback when I set out to parent differently.

My firstborn was the first grandchild in our family, so needless to say, my parents were very authoritarian when expressing their opinions in how I parented. Now let me pause here to say when you become a parent for the first time, I consider it normal to parent the way you are familiar, so there is no parent guilt here. But also, let me give you permission to allow yourself to parent differently at any stage of your parenting journey. It can be done!

## Parenting Differently? Start Where You Are

When you become a parent, did you know you are a parent forever? Meaning you are forever parenting. Meaning you more than likely will have the opportunity to parent your child somehow at every stage of their life, including once they leave your home. Are you parenting differently from your parents? If so, what are your challenges? Do you want to parent differently but think it is too late? It is never too late to parent differently, no matter your children's ages.

Yes, it would be challenging for you and your child because change is hard, but your consistency in parenting with awareness will pay off in significantly positive ways. You are creating a supportive family environment of love, trust, respect, empathy, and effective communication.

I believe in training a child to have good behaviors and mannerisms while he or she is young. Yes, that is an ideal age, and I am aware some parents don't or didn't have that awareness or opportunity when their children were younger. But it is never too late. Start where you are.

Even though my boys are years apart in age, I manage to parent them well from a young age. My firstborn was age 13 when my parenting style was in transition, and I remember discussing with him that I would be parenting differently and letting him know how the changes would affect him. He did not grasp the entire concept (in his mind, he blamed his brothers for the change), but as time went by, he was able to go with the flow. Some days were more challenging than others.

## Suggestions for Starting Now

- Trust yourself.
- Start with small changes — Inform your teenager. Create a routine check-in with self.
- Schedule quality time.

Good practices to help you grasp your parent awareness skill and open communication:

- Know your child's passion and interest
- Encourage them in that area
- Confidently guide and set limits
- Monitor and observe their activities

## Fear, Hesitancy, and Courage

Over the years, I have met and coached parents who knew what actions to take or what words were needed to be spoken to redirect their teen's behavior but lacked the courage and confidence to take immediate action. Fear, lack of effective communication skills, and lack of trust were the reasons. It is here that I encourage parents to be observant of their actions and realize that their child is aware of their hesitancy and can/will use that to manipulate the situation even more.

Parenting with confidence and courage is imperative if we want our teens to get the right message when redirecting their behavior.

When you feel fear and hesitancy in a parenting decision or conversation you must have with your teen, what are your thoughts? How do you get past that moment and proceed with your parental action? Do you call a friend? Journal writing? Pray? Exercise/go for a walk? Talk it out with other family members/partners?

Over the years, when I felt fear and hesitancy in parenting, I also found myself feeling alone. Feeling alone came from me doubting my ability to make the right parental decision at that moment. But over time, I got comfortable with the idea of encouraging and motivating myself.

Although I had mommy friends and family to chat about parenting stuff and my challenges, there came a time when our parenting journeys and experiences started to differ.

How do you encourage yourself when you are in the space of feeling alone in your parenting journey?

Well, here is what I started to do for my sanity: read, journal, reflect, and collect quotes. So, over the years, I used many quotes to help me expand my awareness of how I parent and live day-to-day.

## Here are a few of my favorite quotes and spoken words that put me in a thoughtful space:

- *You have the exact qualities God knew your teen would need in a parent ~ be encouraged.*
- *The children you have attracted into your life are here to mirror to you how you have yet to grow. - Shefali Tsabary*
- *Conscious parenting or parenting with awareness is about improving yourself for the benefit of your children.*
- *"There is no such thing as a perfect parent, so just be a real one." - Sue Atkins*
- *Thinking without awareness is the main dilemma of human existence. - Eckhart Tolle*
- *"It's not one big break that brings success. It's the consistency of your daily disciplines, habits, and routines." - Terri Foy*

## Question to Self:

Do you have any family, or parenting affirmations, mantras, or quotes that you read and get you to self-reflect?

_____

_____

_____

_____

Parenting with awareness is a good foundation for your children and family. Raising your teen with awareness of the family's parenting style, learning style, birth order, and stress triggers is a

great asset for your child to have as they mature into young adults. This allows them to have the awareness and the skill to observe these characteristics in other people and effectively communicate with confidence (workplace, academic and social environments).

## How to Enjoy Your Parenting Years

Learn to parent with self-awareness. Self-awareness is knowing and understanding your own feelings, motives, and desires. When I grasped this concept, I realized that being a good parent to my children required me to be observant of my daily actions and behaviors as an adult. Also, this caused me to be observant of my own childhood emotions that would show up when I was reacting to my child's unacceptable behavior.

I began to enjoy my parenting years around the time my firstborn was graduating high school. Critical points for me, I was starting to understand how my self-awareness and my new way of parenting were creating less stress for me in my day-to-day family dynamics. Why? Because I was learning to be confident in my parenting skills, my ability to be observant of my emotional triggers, and aware of my thoughts as I entertain any given situation.

Here is an example of how I would be responding to a full week of family activities and the daily family stuff in my self-awareness mode. I am in this mode to minimize the stress that I know in advance is a stressful situation.

Meditation was not part of my process at this stage of my life. Still, I was doing the self-talk, which was my way of preparing myself mentally for a week of nonstop driving around the city usually to sporting events. If I did not prepare myself mentally, my children would feel and observe my annoyance and negative vibes. So, I learned to be in the best spirit possible for them to be in their best spirit to participate in their sport.

After much practice, I found ways to be kind to myself during the sporting season, such as reading or buying a good book (reading is one of my favorite things), word search books, treating myself to dinner alone, scheduling dates with my girlfriends, etc.

Another self-awareness moment for me would be to be intentional in being in a good energy space before dropping off and picking up from school. I have known to pick the kids up on several occasions, only to find them in a foul mood. I did not appreciate that, so I was intentional in being in my happy space so that I could happily redirect their unpleasant attitude so that our family evening could go smoothly.

4-awarenesses that helped me shift my parenting skills to the next level: Parenting Styles, Learning Styles, Birth Order, Stress Triggers

1. Understanding my parenting style, I learned to be confident and consistent in family matters.
2. Understanding my family's learning styles helped me to communicate effectively one on one, set appropriate boundaries, and address academic concerns effectively.
3. Understanding my family's birth order was of interest to me because I am the firstborn in my family of five children. I did not enjoy the responsibility of the traditional label of being the oldest. Understanding my sons' birth order helped me be intentional in my interactions with each of them.
4. Understanding my family stress triggers proved to be highly effective during emotional outbursts, family meetings, and setting new boundaries and expectations. Also, I was able to parent my family to know and understand each other's stress triggers.

These 4-awarenesses were vital in helping me create my family flow. Minimize my parenting stress understand, and effectively communicate within my family dynamics. It was not always easy and flowing, but I learned that as the parent, I knew it was my responsibility to be consistent, firm, fair, fun, and flexible as I adjusted to my new way of parenting.

## Parent Support System Is Necessary

Do you have a reliable parent support system? What does that support system look like for your family dynamics?

When I speak of the parent support system, I refer to friends, family, educators, and community programs, including church organizations that support parents and family life development.

Ideally, parental support systems need to consist of responsible adults who are trustworthy, empathetic, and have similar family values.

As a parent facilitator, I often heard parents say they did not know such a program existed. Others wanted to know how to get continued support after the group, and I always found this feedback rewarding. By the end of the six-week session, they were most grateful for the new awareness about their parental attitudes and practices related to their communication and involvement with their teenager.

I encourage parental support because as parents, some days we are at our wits end dealing with adolescents' behavior, and having that outside emotional and practical support from another

trusted parent, adult, and/or friend can help give another perspective on the behavior and resolve any lingering issue or conflict in a timely manner. Also, with a trusted support system in place, please do not rely on them solely for challenging issues but also get their feedback and/or reinforcement for basic social skills learning: this is something all teens need during this stage of their development, such as empathy, expressing feelings, nonverbal communication, being part of a group, caring about others and self, problem-solving, active listening, standing up for self, and managing conflict. All this equates to our teens having positive growth and connection in school and their social lives.

*"The key ingredient in family communication is listening, really listening."*

—— ZIG ZIGLAR

# CHAPTER 5
# FAMILY COMMUNICATION AND AGE GAP

## How We Communicate

Are you an attentive listener? Do you communicate effectively with your teen when redirecting? Are you mindful of the non-verbal cues (words, voice tone, body language)? Improving and maintaining family communication and relationships is a necessary skill for every parent.

In the early years, communication in the Lewis household seemed to be all me (mom). I often wondered whether it was also because I was a boy mom. It felt as if I was always initiating, informing, guiding, directing, etc.: Do this. Do that. Did you do that? Did you do this? As for their response to my directive, I would get one-liner or one-word answers on most occasions.

The limited conversations and responses I was getting from the male species in my household as they got older required me to communicate more directly. If I were persistent with my questioning, I would begin to see and feel their agitation in their response. With my new knowledge about how we communicate, I changed my voice tone, and when I spoke, I was specific and direct. Why? Because I realized they had short attention spans. With this adjustment in how I communicated, I had to practice patience with myself and my family members.

I noticed how my stress-level shifted for the better once I started communicating with my family differently, leading to less yelling and fewer daily lectures.

Before my new way of parenting was in full effect, I noticed my behavior — constantly repeating and redirecting my sons over and over about their daily actions and responsibilities. I could feel the tension and stress in my body at the thought of the actions I needed to take to get things done for the day and deal with their lack of urgency.

During this time, I noticed a behavior pattern where they would wait until I asked for the third or fourth time before moving into action, meaning my sons did not attempt to move on the first or second ask. I resolved this behavior by stating, "If I have to ask a third time, there will be a consequence." Of course, they tested me on this course of action on several occasions. Still, they eventually got the message and started to move more quickly on things, usually after my second request. My daily life became less stressful once my boys saw me be consistent and firm in this action.

## Four Strategies for Effective Family Communication:

BE AN ACTIVE LISTENER...acknowledge and respect the family members' perspective or point of view, also consider the ages and mature level within your family dynamics

PAY ATTENTION...tone and body language, non-verbal messages, and behaviors

COMMUNICATE FREQUENTLY...MAKE TIME, talk in the car, turn TV off, limited use of electronic devices, eat dinner together, family meetings

SHOW RESPECT...two-way street, lack of boundaries invites a lack of respect, clarify what respect means to your family

Effective communication requires everyone to be an active listener. But as parents, we must model what that looks like for our family and help everyone understand the importance of effective communication at home, school, work, and any social environment.

The benefits of effective family communication are strong family trust, open communication, being seen, feeling heard, a safe environment for important and sensitive issues to be discussed, acceptance, and understanding of one another.

## Questions to Self:

Do you think you can create a home environment where your teens would feel safe talking to you about anything?

_____

_____

_____

_____

Would your children say you are a good communicator? How about a good listener?

_____

_____

_____

_____

Are you confident that your child can effectively communicate a concern or issue they might have if you are not around? (Work and/or school environment)

_____

_____

_____

_____

When it comes to communication, we all want to be heard and understood. Our ability to do this depends on listening carefully and being aware of non-verbal cues (words, tone of voice, body language).

## Open Family Communication Suggestions:

- Make time to talk
- Practice patience
- Freely use encouraging words
- Chat in a quiet place with no interruptions
- Give compliments like confetti
- Embrace one on one conversations
- Listen without contradicting and repeat what you heard
- Use a positive tone and body language to communicate what you say
- Help your teen to put words to their emotions
- Be positive and show empathy

Parents, be aware that as you communicate with your children, this is an opportunity for your child to know that your love for them has no limits and is unconditional. So, seize the moment.

## Words to Say Often to Help Your Teen Feel Seen and Heard:

- I love you
- I am proud of you
- I am sorry
- I forgive you
- I am listening

When a parent speaks words of encouragement and validation to their teens, it lets them know they are valued, heard, and seen. Teenagers love hearing these affirming phrases but respect them even more when they come from their parents. I encourage you to seek out moments of opportunities to speak these and other positive words to your child.

## Learning Styles and How We Best Learn

Learning styles are methods you use to process and remember information. Being aware of your learning styles and your child's learning styles can be beneficial to how you parent, especially when communicating and enforcing the boundaries and expectations you have set for your family. As a parent of sons born in the Gen Y or Millennial generation, I want to identify a few learning styles that resonate with them. The millennial generation was born between 1981 and 1996.

- Technology-Savvy Learners: comfortable and proficient in using technology to learn.
- Social learners: benefit from environments where they can work together, share learning experiences, and exchange ideas.
- Visual learners: learn best when using visual aids to assist in their learning process, such as charts, graphs, and videos.
- Experienced learners: learn best when they engage in real-world assignments and can apply what they learned.
- Personalized learners: They appreciate technologies that adapt to their learning style and offer individualized feedback.

Your child will likely exhibit a combination of these learning styles or others not mentioned here, but these are a few of the ones I observed in my children during their school-age years.

Due to the gap in my boys' ages, I saw that they each approached school and classwork differently. When I became aware of learning styles and how we learn best, two of my boys were still in school.

The learning differences between my sons as it relates to homework:

Son #1: Likes doing his homework last minute, on the way to school, or at school

Son #2: Likes doing his homework as soon as he gets home from school

Son #3: Likes doing his homework at night with music

So, with my new awareness about learning styles and how we learn, instead of my insisting that they all do their homework simultaneously in the same area. I created a clear rule about homework with each of them. The rule? I do not care how/when you do your homework as long as it gets done. Of course, when they were younger, I was more hands-on with homework activities. But as they got older, I explained to them the importance of doing their own

homework and my responsibility as the parent to make sure they get it done. That included me asking daily: Do you have homework? What time will you start working on it? Did you finish? This was followed by "Let me review it."

Remember, you are the parenting expert on your child. As parents, it benefits our teenagers and us to know how they learn best and take in information.

Understanding your family's learning styles is a great tool to incorporate into your processes for effectively communicating with your children. Their ability to learn depends upon how they perceive information.

We all have natural strengths, and we all are a blend of learning styles. This awareness can help you know your family member's strengths and guide you through parenting accordingly.

## How We Best Learn:

Average retention rates:

Lecture 5%

Reading 10%

Audio/Visual 20%

Demonstration 30%

Discussion Group 50%

Practice by Doing 75%

Teach Others 90%

*Adapted from National Training Laboratories. Bethel, Maine*

I want you as the parent to be genuinely confident in your parenting style. Be courageous and prepare in advance mentally and emotionally for the things you know will be approaching in the different stages of your parenting, such as lying, stealing, cheating, missing curfew, skipping class/school, hanging out with the wrong crowd, bullied/bullying, smoking, or showing low academic progress — to name a few. But also prepare yourself for the excellent behavior of your child as well, such as being honest, responsible, dependable, caring, respectful, having good grades and time management skills. Both groups of behavior need to be acknowledged.

> *"If a child cannot learn the way we teach, maybe we should teach the way they learn."*
>
> - IGNACIO ESTRADA

## Family Meetings & Stress Triggers

Family meetings are an excellent way to keep open communication within your home environment. It is also a good family tradition for your children and their children. Family

meetings can be fun and without conflict. I would suggest having meetings to touch base and update the family on anything relating to the dynamic of your household and any persistent behavior issues that present themselves. A good family meeting can take place in under 30 minutes. Set clear boundaries and ground rules and be mindful of family members' attention spans by speaking directly to the point using the strategies we discussed in the "How We Communicate" section. Also, consider the emotion attached to any family feedback during these meetings, such as anger, fear, sadness, guilt, shame, or discomfort.

Family meetings at my house usually occurred when I had seen unacceptable behaviors become repetitive even after multiple verbal warnings over time. Our family meetings were usually interactive, meaning I would state the reason for the meeting to clarify or reframe boundaries and expectations. Next, I would allow them to ask me questions or give feedback. One son was always very talkative doing the meeting, and the other two would answer questions if directed at them. On occasion, emotions were visible, and usually that related to sibling rivalry. This would lead to my explaining the age differences and maturity level once again related to adjustments of a specific family rule/boundary.

Awareness of your teens' stress triggers is another effective parenting strategy. It is no secret that teens are stressed, depressed, and emotionally charged. As I write this, we are living in a pandemic—stressful times for our families and our society.

The most common stress triggers for teens are school/academics, social connection, family conflict, expectations, traumatic events, and life changes in family dynamics. Physical symptoms of stress can be headaches, skin problems, teeth grinding, nail-biting, stomach upset/nausea, tight neck/shoulder, shortness of breath, and foot/finger tapping, to name a few.

## Question to Self:

What are your stress triggers? How do they show up physically for you?

_____

_____

_____

_____

_____

Are you familiar with your teenager's stress triggers? Do you know what emotions are attached to their stress?

_____

_____

_____

_____

_____

To genuinely connect and support your teenager in this way, you, the parent, must communicate, listen, and be empathetic.

I encourage you to be observant of the stress triggers in your family dynamics and use your parenting strategies to deal with them.

I remember a time and season of my parenting journey when I was stressed and did not realize it until I had gone to several doctors for back and shoulder pain, and they ran all kinds of tests only to tell me everything looked normal. They asked me about my daily interactions with work and home life, concluded I was stressed and over-exerting myself, and suggested that I stop doing so much. That was laughable to me because my third son was a toddler. It was then that I began reading about stress and its effects on the body. Of course, I made some changes in my lifestyle, but I was in awe of the physical symptoms stress can cause in one's body. Another adjustment I made in my lifestyle was communicating with my children when I felt at my limit, stressed, and needed to rest physically.

When they became teenagers, I was more intentional in telling them when I was stressed and how it affected me at that moment. This sometimes led them to be more cooperative in getting things done but not always.

Also, I saw this as an opportunity and teachable moment to explain what stress is and how it can affect your body. My physical symptoms during that time were migraines and back pain.

So, be empathetic when communicating with your teen about stress and the symptoms. Share in some way how you can relate to being stressed. Usually, our children know when we are stressed, but my intention is to encourage you, the parent, to have the conversation. I have heard so many teens in my parenting class talk about what stresses them out. And when asked if they discussed this with their parents, the majority of the time, the answer would be "No, they won't listen" or "No, they don't understand." Teenagers do think parents don't understand. Usually, that relates to us not being good listeners.

You might already know your teen's stress triggers and physical symptoms, but are you effectively communicating with them to minimize health risks and keep family communication lines open?

## Age Gap

With my sons' age gap, I quickly learned the importance of one-on-one time, and the opportunity to show them they are loved, seen, and heard as individuals. There is a seven and six-year age gap between my sons. Of course, I have seen families with more significant age gaps, and I have wondered how effective communication is in their household.

One of my biggest challenges in parenting with such an age gap was planning activities that worked for all three ages.

Having my boys spaced out in age did create parenting breaks for me. But looking at the big picture, it seemed like I was forever parenting. I felt like my parenting days were being extended, which led me to be longer in the taxi mom club than I desired. This became a verified truth when I found myself parenting a teenager while in menopause. Oh My God! These two do not go together. You have been forewarned.

I developed strategies that helped me minimize my stress at any given moment as a parent with multiple age gaps. I learned to be flexible and creative in my parenting style, have realistic expectations for myself and my family, and be patient. These strategies help me focus on the family memories that were being created.

As I became more confident in my new way of parenting, my awareness muscle got more vigorous. This led me to see the unique differences in my boys clearly, and I parented accordingly.

## Characteristics of My Boys I Learned to Embrace While Parenting:

Son #1: Quiet, stubborn, takes time to warm up to things and people, gets upset quickly, resists change, moody, misbehave, gentle, temperamental, driven and motivated as most, has his way of being in the world, his unique personality.

Son #2: Soft-spoken, friendly, resistant to change, moody, gentle, temperamental, has his way of being in the world, his unique personality.

Son #3: He is talkative, friendly, can misbehave, deviant, dramatic, finds it hard to sit still, has his way of being in the world, and is his unique person.

## Question to Self:

What are the different characteristics you see in your teenager?

_____

_____

_____

_____

_____

_____

_____

_____

_____

_____

Parenting three sons with significant age gaps allowed me the experience to reinvent my parenting wheel three times and live to talk about it. Parenting is forever; therefore, I have written this book.

## Family Care and Family Values

Family values are about knowing who we are so we can build connections within our family dynamic. Family values describe the roles, beliefs, ideals, and attitudes you desire your family to demonstrate in their everyday life.

Your teenagers must know the values you have for them so they can solidify the bond you desire for your family.

**Lewis Household Family Values**: Love, compassion, communication, responsibility, honesty, forgiveness, respect, help each other, you belong, be yourself, do your best, memories, traditions, be flexible, attitude is everything, be friendly, smile, say sorry, pray, trust God, never give up.

## Question to Self:

Do your children know your family values? If not, create a list and have a family meeting to discuss. Have fun!

_____

_____

_____

_____

Family care can look different in all families. Family care to a parent is 24/7, and I want to shine awareness on how it can include parents being intentional and having a plan to raise teenagers who display positive characteristics and strong social skills. We must parent with the awareness that our teens hear what we say but focus more on our actions and reactions. We are their example and role model for them being their best self during their teen years and beyond.

## Question to Self:

What does family care look like in your home?

_____

_____

_____

_____

## Lessons I Purposely Instilled in My Sons Before High School:

- ⊙ be kind and respectful to others
- ⊙ they do have a voice; they are comfortable with it; they know how to voice their opinion without having a temper tantrum
- ⊙ they understand what being responsible feels and looks like
- ⊙ it is okay to ask for help; you do not know everything; and it is okay
- ⊙ family matters, make time for family

- ⟩ enjoy life, it is not all work, create memories
- ⟩ pray, trust God, know that God speaks and hears them
- ⟩ how to say silent prayers throughout their day
- ⟩ it is okay to fail; learn the lesson and move on
- ⟩ life is hard, and I had to learn it on my own (I would share a personal story for encouragement)
- ⟩ it is okay to motivate yourself
- ⟩ they have parents that understand their struggles we were once their age

## Question to Self:

What life lessons are you purposely instilling in your teenager?

_____

_____

_____

_____

*"Disconnection doesn't occur when there's dissent, but when there's intolerance of each other's differences."*

—— SHEFALI TSABARY

# CHAPTER 6
# FAMILY LOVE LANGUAGE AND BIRTH ORDER

## How We Love

During my boys' elementary school years, I intentionally did fun things and spent quality time with them. At this age, I could still plan things that all of them enjoyed.

But as they entered the pre-teen years, I had to be creative and flexible in planning my quality time with them. Why? Different interests, sports, academic schedules, and social events.

Planned family quality time would include all three boys; one would be "bored," one just "okay," and one "happy." After several family outings like this, I started to notice a pattern. So going forward, I would inform them of the family activity and get feedback. Eventually, I started a rotating schedule of which family members got to choose the quality time outing, and I encouraged everyone to be happy.

Also, with this new awareness, I decided to be more intentional in spending one-on-one time with each at least once during the week. The weekends were usually filled with sports.

One-on-one time for me was a 15–30 minute intentional connection. I would focus on what they had to say even when they were not talkative. I usually had inquiry questions about what I wanted to know related to their teen world, and I made my expectation known that they respond with more than "one word."

It was not until I read Gary Chapman's book *The Five Love Languages of Teenagers* that I became more confident in planning quality time with each of them, and I now knew their specific love language. This was my guide for being observant and intentional during our times together.

## The Five Love Languages of Teenagers:

- Words of affirmation
- Physical touch
- Quality time
- Acts of service
- Gifts

Lewis family primary love language:

*My first born—Words of affirmation*
*My middle son—Quality time*
*My youngest son—Gifts*

Our one-on-one quality time included something they enjoyed doing and fun. How much time should you spend as quality time? That can vary, so consider your family dynamics and remember the parent's goal is to connect in meaningful ways.

## Quality Time vs. Quantity Time

Children need both quality time and quantity time from parents.

There was a phase of my parenting journey where I focused on quantity time with my sons — being there wherever "there" was for them. Making sure they saw and felt my presence and support.

I always describe my parenting journey as being on a daily rollercoaster, mainly because of the age gap. I was always planning, picking up, dropping off, traveling from one practice/game after another but not genuinely spending quality time with each son. I feel safe to say my family was getting plenty quantity time.

I have heard many parents say they don't have enough time, and I have listened to children say my parents are always tired, work late, and are busy with siblings. This can easily be the messages you are hearing now from your teen, and if so, I suggest you reprioritize your time, be creative in your schedule planning, and carve out that quality time. Find the balance between quality time and quantity time.

Once I grasped the awareness that children value quality time as much as quantity time with their parents, I began to question and observe how my sons viewed the time we were together.

## Question to Self:

My primary love language is words of affirmation and quality time. What is yours?

_____

_____

_____

_____

Do you think knowing your child's primary love language would help you build a stronger connection?

_____

_____

_____

_____

Do you currently have a balance of quality time and quantity time with your family?

_____

_____

_____

_____

## Birth Order Matters — At Least for Me, It Did

Awareness of birth order can be important. I am a firstborn with four siblings, and I was never comfortable being called the oldest because I never understood why the oldest was responsible for younger siblings' behavior.

When I learned about birth order, it was during my years when I was facilitating parent classes for truancy court. Parents would seek advice on how to handle their teens' behavior related to conflict with their siblings. When I would respond by asking sibling ages most of the time, there was an age gap. But they would also refer to their children in birth order (my firstborn, middle child, my youngest, my next to the youngest).

Although the topic of birth order was not part of the curriculum, I offered suggestions because of my own experience as the firstborn of my family and my age gap situation going on with my boys. But as I thought more about the issues, I decided to research the effects of birth order in general. That's when I discovered *The Birth Order Book* by Dr. Kevin Leman.

I was very familiar with the conflict they were describing with their teen, such as resentment, bitterness, anger, being rude to siblings, sibling rivalry, not feeling part of the family dynamic, and behavior issues at home and school.

I learned that siblings might grow up in the same family, but they do not all experience the family environment in the same way. I believe birth order and age differences play a role in that.

## Birth Order and Personality Type

Awareness of birth order and personality type is another strategy to use when being creative in making effective connections with your teenager. Dr. Leman gives details about the various personality types in his book. So, here I will share how the birth order relates to my family.

- Firstborn Child (surrogate parent) protective, responsible, natural leader, ambitious, responsible, and authoritarian
- Middle Child (peacekeeper) tend to lean on their friends, social butterfly, negotiator, insightful, independent, and passive
- Youngest Child (charming rebel) less rules-oriented, free spirit

My three sons fit into these main categories perfectly. However, I have seen my middle son take on the characteristics of the firstborn over the years, and I now know why this behavior showed up in my experience. Dr. Leman states, "when there is a gap of seven to ten years or more, the next child falls into the "quasi-only child" category." He also states, "When there is a five- to six-year gap between children, the next child starts a 'new family.'" I can clearly see over time how each of my sons has displayed "firstborn" tendencies.

I realize there are different family dynamics than mine and other variables to consider when talking about birth order, such as age gap, gender, temperament, and uniqueness. Research the topic on birth order and see how you can use this awareness to connect more with your teenager.

Birth order tips to help your child feel equally loved and self-confident:

- Learn how to reassure and express you have enough love for all your children.
- Avoid forcing perfection.
- Share your birth order experience.
- Create moments where you share photo/video memories where you were loving and attentive to them at various stages of their growing years.
- Have the conversation and be observant of anger or jealousy of younger siblings.
- Create an environment where they are safe talking about their emotions.
- Help each child develop a sense of self by participating in activities they enjoy.

I used my understanding of how birth order related to each of my sons to create effective conversations when we did have those moments where I was all ears.

## Question to Self:

Do you think understanding your child's birth order would help you parent or communicate differently?

_____

_____

_____

_____

_____

_____

How do you feel about your birth order in your family? Would you feel comfortable sharing that experience with your child?

_____

_____

_____

_____

_____

_____

"*You don't always know what your kids will do, but your kids should always know what you will do.*"

— JOYCE SANDERS

# CHAPTER 7
# FAMILY BOUNDARIES AND EXPECTATIONS

## Boundaries & Expectations

Boundaries and expectations should be a part of every family dynamic. It creates an environment of expectation for every family member to know what is expected. The most effective way to enforce these rules is with love, respect, and empathy.

When I started to change my parenting style and was intentional in being firm and consistent with the boundaries and expectations, it was stressful and challenging for several reasons:

1. Boundaries in my parents' household when I was growing up were constantly changing without notice, meaning I knew about boundaries but was not familiar with them being consistent.
2. There was a large age gap between my sons.
3. I did not feel supported.

As I later grew confident in parenting with clear boundaries, I was able to see how being firm and consistent in enforcing them created an environment for them to be familiar with our family boundaries easily.

What are family boundaries? They are clearly understood rules parents create for their family to provide structure and routine. They are protective, appropriate, and can, on occasion, include compromise and flexibility. Being flexible and compromising in this area of my parenting journey was a part of me minimizing my stress.

When asked if they could sleep over at a friend's house and I had no advance notification, my response would be NO because the rule was that I had to know ahead of time to coordinate with the hosting parent. Of course, I was the meanest mother; they thought it would be an easy YES since I knew the parent/family. Yes, there was pouting and the silent treatment, but once I addressed this behavior, I would remind them of our family rule "advance notification" and why that rule was created. After making sure the rule was understood, I suggested a compromise by giving permission to set up a sleepover date for a future time.

## The Benefits of Family Boundaries:

- everyone learns to say "yes" confidently and "no"
- respect, everyone learns to listen and respond to authority
- security, everyone develops a stronger sense of safety
- enjoyment, everyone recognizes the firm and consistent expectation of the household and can focus on fun and enjoyment

Boundaries and expectations are not one-size-fits-all. Different children and situations often require different rules and consequences.

## Question to Self:

Are you comfortable with the idea of working together with your teen to come up with guidelines that let all family members know what is expected and what is not in the best interest of the family?

_____

_____

_____

_____

Do you involve your teenager in setting boundaries and deciding the consequence?

_____

_____

_____

_____

Do you take the time to explain to your teenager why you set the boundaries that exist in your household?

_____

_____

_____

_____

If you asked your teen what he or she expected of you as a parent, what do you think the response would be?

_____

_____

_____

_____

Boundaries and expectations are a necessary discussion because of the busy lifestyles we all live nowadays. Our teens must know the family boundaries and expectations for important issues such as dating, sex, drugs, respecting self, and others, driving, etc. When it came to my boys'

getting cars and driving, I admit I had a constant knot in my stomach, or you can say a ball of fear, even after driving school and passing the driving test. Later came the car accidents and traffic tickets.

Family rules and expectations for my teenage drivers:

1. Only two passengers plus yourself.
2. No speeding or texting.
3. Traffic tickets are your responsibility.
4. No one can drive your car.
5. Having a car did not mean no curfew.

It has been my experience that children, especially teenagers, think our rules/boundaries are unfair. That is only because they cannot see or feel the love in our expectations. Neither can they understand that, as parents, it is our responsibility to protect them.

Parents, trust yourself and know that teenagers do better in life when rules are clear, consistent, and fair. When it comes to setting limits, it will feel uncomfortable and can be challenging, especially when dealing with various age groups within a household.

Because of my sons' age differences, there were various times and many things that did not apply to all three sons at one time. (Constant battle for them and me.)

I had a genius moment years ago, and it was my solution to limit the dialogue and unwelcome feedback I received when they thought I was unfair. I would ask a simple question when they felt the rules were unfair. That required them to stop talking and think, "How old are you?" or "What's your age?" It was like a light bulb moment in their immature brain when they answered my question and reflected on the unfair rule. Yup! I got good at reminding my boys of their ages.

There was always conflict around what the other brother was or was not doing and why. Eventually, they became aware of age-appropriate conversation through me using this strategy.

When parents set clear boundaries, it helps our teenagers know what to expect.

Here are some expectations (not always spoken) that every teenager eventually has about their parents or other adults in their life.

They want to know that as their parent, we watch out for their safety, respect them as a young adult, take pride in helping them grow to be individual, set appropriate boundaries, challenge them to succeed, expect them to do their best, comfort them when they fail, and help them learn about the world.

## Parent Guilt and Setting Boundaries

Do you feel guilty when setting boundaries? Is it a challenge for you to be firm with the consequences when family rules are broken? I know I did.

There were so many moments when I was overwhelmed with guilt. Early in my parenting years, I would feel guilty for leaving my baby at the daycare. I worked long hours and was too tired to do anything fun, especially when they were elementary age and still had energy after coming home from school. I also went through a stage where I felt guilt for yelling so much. On occasion, they would yell back and say, "Why are you yelling?" but "in my defense," sometimes it was justifiable because I felt ignored. I admit there were times when the yelling was a bit much for the behavior I was redirecting. As I learned how to parent with awareness, I learned how to respond to my family differently. Over time, I managed my guilt by embracing calm and being firm and consistent with family boundaries, creating positive results.

It is okay! Create a new boundary or revise the current one. When it comes to boundaries and limits, every teenager needs consistency and parents who can teach and guide them. Even if they act mature for their age, they still need parental guidance. So be confident when reinforcing your family boundaries and expectations.

Feeling guilty about parenting decisions is known to be a part of the parenting process, but I encourage you not to let your guilt be used to limit your actions as a parent. As I write this, we are in a pandemic, and most children are home and homeschooled. Have you experienced any guilt in setting boundaries during this time?

Guilt can leave you feeling overwhelmed and exhausted. Let it go, forgive yourself, show yourself some grace.

Many times during your parenting journey, parent guilt will show up. I suggest you be intentional with yourself, have a moment of stillness, and ask, "Why do I feel guilty over this parenting decision?" These moments allow you to see how you can let go of the guilt or minimize its stress.

It is okay to give yourself permission to let go of parent guilt and embrace being intentional in taking the time to develop the parenting skills you need to raise your teenager to be emotionally healthy, socially mature, and responsible with as little guilt as possible. You are parenting with awareness.

## Steps to create family boundaries:

- Make it clear.
- Identify categories.
- Keep the list short and simple.
- Set dates.
- Display list.

Make it clear from the beginning that you want everyone to contribute, but you as the parent will have the final word. When identifying categories, be creative here as it relates to your family dynamics and family values such as respect, honesty, responsibility, compassion, courage, and perseverance. Keep the list short and simple by starting with three main boundaries for each category relevant to your family's foundational needs. Others can be added later. Set an effective date when your new boundaries will take effect, giving everyone ample opportunity to be informed, to help everyone stay informed and have a visual display of the "family boundaries" list. They can be displayed inside each bedroom next to the light switch, bathroom mirror, or refrigerator. Be creative. I put mine on the refrigerator, and everyone knew they were there and saw me read them out loud when they seemed to have a memory lapse.

## Things to remember during this process:

- Be patient and calm (will test new boundaries/limits)
- Be firm and consistent as a parent is key, and it is a great way to set the standards of expectations because inconsistency can send the wrong message.
- Negotiate new boundaries as your teen grows older (explain the change calmly and with empathy).

⊙ Respect your teen's need for privacy (at this age, they are seeking more freedom).

I encourage you to take from this book only what applies to your family dynamics, what is relevant to you and your child; be creative, be flexible, and know that all family environments are different. My goal is to help minimize your parenting stress and help you enjoy your parenting years.

Parents, you help your teenagers be the best they can be when your expectations for them are both high and reasonable. There needs to be a balance. High expectations may cause your child to be anxious about living up to your standards. Too low expectations may cause your child to feel you don't believe in them.

I want parents to know they are not alone in trying to be consistent in creating boundaries and expectations for their children. Setting limits for our family is a stressful task, and no parent should feel bad for seeking support. Asking or accepting help shows your courage and awareness in recognizing that sometimes parents do not have all the answers, and it is okay.

## Question to Self:

Do you have expectations for yourself? Do others have expectations of you?

_____

_____

_____

_____

What would the conversation look like if you shared your expectations for yourself with your teen?

_____

_____

_____

_____

Have you ever shared with your teen the goals and boundaries you have for yourself? Ex: work, home, friend, etc.

_____

_____

_____

_____

Have you ever shared with your teen a time when you were younger or as an adult when a family member or non-family member believed in you and challenged you to be your best?

_____

_____

_____

_____

These self-reflection questions are valuable because teenagers need to be confident in setting boundaries and limits for themselves. At the same time, being respectful of the boundaries and expectations set by their parents. They need to see parents and other trusted adults in their environment who demonstrates and teach by example regarding boundaries and expectations. They also need our feedback.

As parents, we need to be aware of those moments when our teenagers need encouragement to keep going when they do not meet our expectations. Let's get into the practice of assuring them that we are cheering them on even as they learn to master the skills of boundaries, setting limits, and having expectations.

Healthy family relationships are built on healthy family boundaries.

*"To shift to a more effective way of relating to our children, we must be willing to face and resolve issues in ourselves that stem from the way we were parented."*

—— SHEFALI TSABARY

# CONCLUSION

## Bringing It All Together

Parenting knowledge and education are part of a parent's development to nurture and respond to the diverse needs of their teenager. Today, I inspire some and give permission to others to create new boundaries and expectations, identify personal parenting styles, learn how to flow with life changes, and effectively communicate. When raising families, change is complicated and sometimes even painful. Still, it's part of parenting and helping our children be their best while keeping them safe and healthy.

Parents, I am proud of you. Thank you for reading my book. As you read how my parenting journey unfolded, it was the evolving of suppressed emotion triggered by my sons' behavior to learning self-awareness and practicing new habits and behaviors that contributed to my personal growth while giving my sons the guidance and room to grow. Yes, most days, it was a balancing act. No, it was not an overnight change. But I was encouraged because I felt less stressed.

I hope you find the courage and confidence to parent differently and well, no matter what stage you are in on your parenting journey. By now, you should be able to see where you are in your parenting journey, know which parenting skill needs improvement, and which strategy will best fit you and your teenager. I believe every parent can learn to enjoy their parenting years with their teenager. Being aware and knowing of their developmental milestones and the behavioral changes during this time is a great place to start.

Determine what kind of parent you want to be and do it confidently. Determine your parenting style and what works best for your family dynamics, and trust yourself. It is no secret that parenting teenagers can trigger all kinds of emotional concerns for both parent and teenager.

The collective goal is to raise teenagers who know how to be self-confident, respectful, responsible, and empathetic and can communicate their needs well. The teen you are loving today will soon be your adult child, and you want them to have the knowledge and skill to survive their life uncertainties, meet their responsibilities, and reach their goals.

Although I speak from the perspective of parenting teenagers in this book, the strategies, suggestions, and parenting tips can be adjusted for all school-age children.

Use what applies to you and discard the rest. Let go of any overwhelmed or anxiety you may feel at incorporating these practical but powerful tools into your parenting style. I used them all, and over time I noticed how my parental stress became less. You got this!

Since retiring from public education, I have enjoyed facilitating parent classes for various community organizations helping parents have meaningful, guided conversations about what matters most to them and their families. During our time together, I seek to provide education and share my knowledge of family communication and connection and its importance in parenting. My sons are young adults now, and I am proud of how they show up in the world as confident, respectful, responsible, and caring human beings.

I envision an environment where parents are not ashamed, embarrassed, critical, or guilt-driven to ask or seek help to parent better. I encourage you to parent your best because parenting is forever.

Let's stay in touch. I want to hear which ideas and strategies you chose to incorporate into your family dynamics. If this book has helped you in any way, I want to hear about that too.

www.instagram.com/theforeverparentingproject.com
https://www.facebook.com/Glorialewisparenting